# Avoiding Drugs

by Patricia J. Murphy

Series consultants: Sonja Green, MD, and
Distinguished Professor Emerita Ann Nolte, PhD,
Department of Health Sciences, Illinois State University

Lerner Publications Company • Minneapolis

*For my nephew, Erik (a.k.a. Alex), and my niece, Olivia—Love, Auntie Patty*

The author would like to thank Mathea Falco, president of Drug Strategies; Dominic Cappello; Robert Schwebel, PhD; and Joel Spivak and Daniel E. McGoldrick with the Campaign for Tobacco-Free Kids, as well as countless others for their assistance in the research of this book. In addition, she would like to thank her editor, Catherine Creswell, for her enthusiasm for and support of this project.

Lerner Publications Company
A division of Lerner Publishing Group
241 First Avenue North
Minneapolis, MN 55401 U.S.A.

Website address: www.lernerbooks.com

Words in **bold type** are explained in a glossary on page 31.

Library of Congress Cataloging-in-Publication Data

Murphy, Patricia J., 1963–
    Avoiding drugs / by Patricia J. Murphy.
      p.   cm. – (Pull ahead books)
    Includes index.
    ISBN-13: 978–0–8225–2867–8 (lib. bdg. : alk. paper)
    ISBN-10: 0–8225–2867–3 (lib. bdg. : alk. paper)
    1. Drugs—Juvenile literature. 2. Drug abuse—Juvenile
literature. 3. Drugs of abuse—Juvenile literature. I. Title. II.
Series.
RM301.17.M87 2006
362.29–dc22               2004028889

Manufactured in the United States of America
1 2 3 4 5 6 – JR – 11 10 09 08 07 06

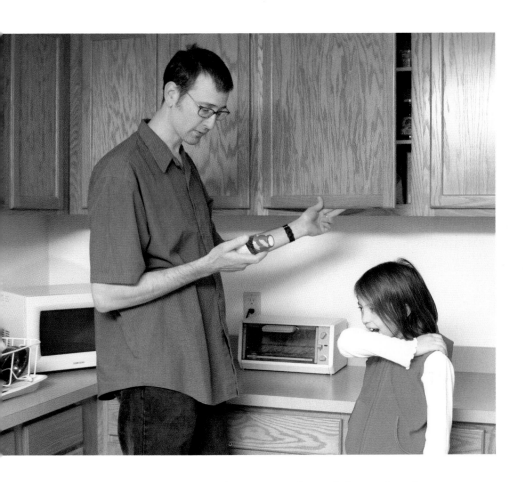

Olivia has a bad cough.  Her father gives her cough **medicine.**

Olivia's medicine is an **over-the-counter drug.** It will help stop Olivia's cough.

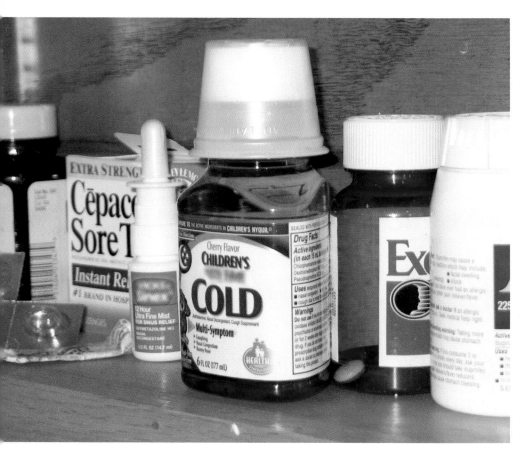

Her father buys it at the store. What over-the-counter drugs can you find at the store?

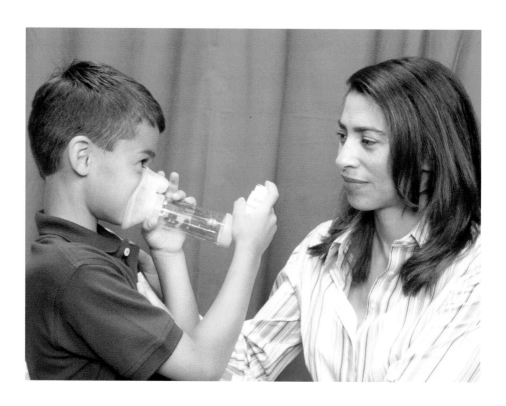

Alex has **asthma**. His mother gives him asthma medicine. Alex's medicine is a **prescription** drug. It will help Alex when he has trouble breathing.

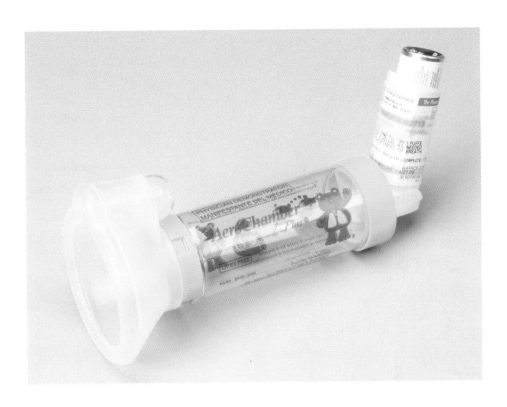

Alex's doctor orders the drug for him.
The medicine is only for Alex. His
mother buys it at the prescription
counter at the store.

Olivia and Alex only take medicine their parents or doctors give them. Their parents read and follow the directions.

The right amount of medicine can help them get well. The wrong amount or the wrong medicine could hurt them!

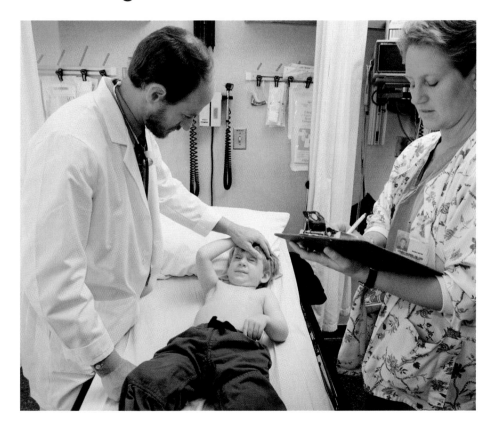

Medicines and vitamins are drugs. Drugs change the way your body works.

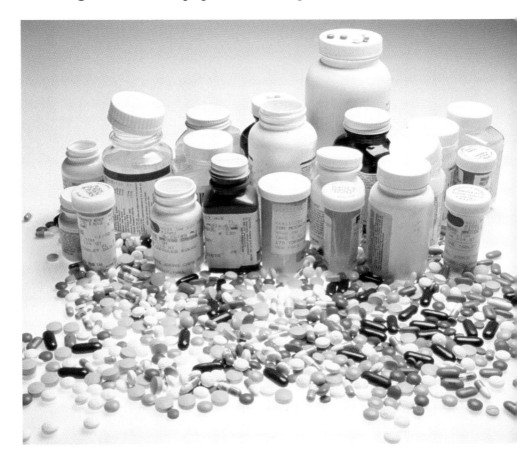

Some drugs help you stay healthy. Others help you when you are sick. These drugs are called **medicinal drugs.**

Some drugs won't help you stay healthy.  They may even hurt your body or make you sick.  These drugs are called **non-medicinal drugs.**

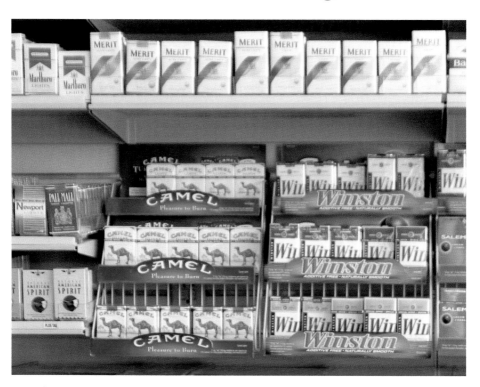

SURGEON GENERAL'S WARNING:
Smoking By Pregnant Women May
Result in Fetal Injury, Premature
Birth, And Low Birth Weight.

**Alcohol** and **nicotine** are non-medicinal
drugs. They can be harmful to the body.
They may cause illness and even death.

Some people **misuse** these or other drugs. They might take drugs when they are sad, lonely, or bored.

They hope the drugs will change the way they feel. But often the drugs make them very sick. Sometimes people can't stop using drugs!

Tommy's grandma smokes cigarettes.
Most days, she coughs a lot.  She also
has trouble breathing.

Tommy
wonders why
she smokes.
Do you know
why?

Cigarettes have **tobacco.** Tobacco has nicotine. It makes it hard for people to stop smoking.

Tobacco can cause lung cancer and other illnesses.

At parties, Sue's aunt always has a drink in her hand. She talks loudly and acts silly. Sometimes she falls down.

Why do you
think Sue's aunt
acts this way?

Her aunt drinks too much alcohol.  Drinks like beer and wine have alcohol.  Alcohol changes how people feel and act.

Drinking too much alcohol makes some
people feel sad. It can make others
feel angry. Over time, too much
alcohol can hurt the body and mind.

Most adults can drink some alcohol and stop.  Others, like Sue's aunt, can't stop.  They need help!

People who drink alcohol and drive can hurt or kill themselves and others. Drinking and driving is against the law.

It's everyone's job to be smart about
drugs. Olivia and Alex take only
the drugs their parents and doctors
give to them.

Olivia and Alex stay away from non-medicinal drugs. You can too!

# What I've Learned

- Only take medicine your parents, a trusted adult, or doctor gives you.

- The wrong medicine or wrong amount of medicine can hurt you.

- Some drugs are not medicine. They do not help you stay healthy. Nicotine and alcohol are these kinds of drugs.

- Nicotine makes it hard to stop smoking.

- Alcohol can make people feel and act differently. Alcohol makes it hard for some people to stop drinking it.

- Some people misuse drugs when they feel bad. Sometimes they can't stop using drugs.

- Drinking and driving is against the law.

# Have a Drug-Free Plan

A friend may ask you to try drugs. Learn how to say no. Practice these lines with someone.

**Person 1:** Want to smoke?
**Person 2:** No, way! I like breathing.

**Person 1:** Try this drug. It will make you feel great.
**Person 2:** I like the way I feel. Drugs only make you feel sick!

**Person 1:** Come on. Have a drink. It'll make you do silly things.
**Person 2:** No, thanks! I like being myself.

**Person 1:** Try this drug. Everybody's doing it!
**Person 2:** No, not everyone's doing it—because I'm NOT doing it.

**Person 1:** If you were my friend, you'd do this drug with me.
**Person 2:** If you keep doing drugs, I can't be your friend!

# Books and Websites

## Books

Bryant-Mole, Karen. *Talking about Drugs*. Austin, TX: Raintree Steck-Vaughn Publishers, 2000.

MacGregor, Cynthia. *Refuse to Use*. New York: Rosen Publishing Group, 2003.

Murphy, Patricia J. *Staying Happy*. Lerner Publications Company, 2006.

Westcott, Patsy. *Why Do People Take Drugs?* Austin, TX: Raintree Steck-Vaughn Publishers, 2001.

## Websites

*KidsHealth*
  *http://www.kidshealth.org/kids*

*Resources for Parents and Teachers, American Council for Drug Education*
  *http://www.acde.org/youth*

*Can We Talk?*
  *http://www.canwetalk.org*

*National Institute on Drug Abuse, National Institute of Health*
  *http://www.nida.nih.gov*

# Glossary

**alcohol:** a liquid found in drinks like wine or beer

**asthma:** a condition that can cause trouble breathing

**medicinal drugs:** drugs that can keep the body healthy or treat illness

**medicine:** a drug used to treat an illness

**misuse:** to use something the wrong way

**nicotine:** a drug found in tobacco and in cigarettes, chaw, and cigars

**non-medicinal drugs:** drugs that affect the body but that do not treat an illness

**over-the-counter drug:** a drug that can be bought without a doctor's order

**prescription:** a doctor's order for a drug

**tobacco:** leaves of the tobacco plant used for smoking or chewing

# Index

**Photo Acknowledgments**

The photographs in this book appear courtesy of: © Todd Strand/Independent Picture Service, front cover, pp. 3, 4, 6, 7, 8, 13, 16, 17, 18, 20, 21, 22, 23, 26, 27; © Sam Lund/Independent Picture Service, p. 5; © Royalty-Free/ CORBIS, pp. 9, 11, 14; PhotoDisc Royalty Free by Getty Images, pp. 10, 15, 19, 24, 25; © Rick Friedman/ CORBIS, p. 12.